Goldfish and Rose

Robert Hershon

Hanging Loose Press
Brooklyn, New York

Published by Hanging Loose Press, 231 Wyckoff Street, Brooklyn, New York 11217-2208. All rights reserved. No part of this book may be reproduced without the publisher's written permission, except for brief quotations in reviews.

www.hangingloosepress.com

Printed in the United States of America
10 9 8 7 6 5 4 3 2 1

Hanging Loose Press thanks the Literature Program of the New York State Council on the Arts for a grant in support of the publication of this book.

Cover art: © Rackstraw Downes, courtesy of Betty Cuningham Gallery, New York. Collection of The Cleveland Museum of Art. *Under the Gowanus on Hamilton Avenue, 1999.* Four-part painting, oil on canvas. Part three: *At the Corner of Court St. Looking South-East.* 18 1/4 x 31 1/4 inches.

Cover design: Marie Carter

Acknowledgments: *American Poetry Review, Agriculture Reader, The Awl, Boog City, The Brooklyn Rail, Court Green, Hanging Loose, The New York Times, The North, OR, Ozone Park, The Recluse,* and *Vanitas.* "Afterword: Grant Avenue" appeared on the website of The Poetry Foundation. Some poems previously appeared in *A Blue Shovel* (Hanging Loose Press). My thanks to Rackstraw Downes for allowing me to use his painting and to Star Black for the gift of her photography; to Joanna Beer and Zoe Donaldson for their help in preparing the manuscript and, as always, to my redoubtable co-editors Dick Lourie, Mark Pawlak, Marie Carter, and the indispensible Donna Brook.

ISBN 978-1-934909-30-0

Library of Congress cataologing-in-publication available on request.

For Sue Levine

"I, who have no brothers or sisters, look with some degree of innocent envy on those who may be said to be born to friends."—James Boswell

Contents

LAST NIGHT THE WIND CAME IN

last night the wind came in
last night the wind came in
it blew through the room
it turned the pages of the book
it blew the socks off the table
it blew the sheets away
it blew the light bulbs out
it blew the cat's whiskers off
it blew the laces out of the boots
it blew the wives out of the beds
it blew the children out of their childhoods
it blew the buttons out of the buttonholes
it blew the letters out of the envelopes
it blew the skin off the places near the bone
last night the wind came in
it blew the pictures out of the frames
it blew the roses out of the cheeks
it blew the keys off the typewriter
it blew the rings off the fingers bells off the toes
it blew upstairs and downstairs
through the keyholes and the cracks in the walls
it left everything leaning one way or the other
it blew through the grease in the oven
and the ice in the freezer
it blew over the place of the horrible
realization and the place of the bitter recrimination
and the place of the decision to try to get out
it bent the toothbrush bristles this way
and the hairbrush bristles that way
it blew the bodies out of these arms
and into those arms
last night the wind came in
it blew the arms all over the room
it blew the eyes to rolling wildly
it blew the hairs off the body
it left everything shivering and unsure
it rose and it fell and it doubled back
and it didn't miss a corner or a turn
and in the morning
the wind came in

and it blew away the daytime
and it blew away up and down
and it blew away hot and cold in and out
far and near good and bad sooner and later
it blew away these words these voices
it left the sound of itself
the whisper and the promise
and the certainty of wind

PACE

on skinny old
lexington avenue
i speed up
to pass this man

so i can
slow down

i take
great pleasure
in the exact size
of my steps

GOLDFISH AND ROSE

An old man sits cross-legged on
the Boulevard Saint Germain and displays
his art on a white cloth: roses carved from
beets and goldfish carved from carrots.
People stop to admire them, but he
does not speak. He holds a beet
and a knife.

Two nights later, he is showing the same
roses and the same goldfish and the beet
he is holding is still entirely a beet.
What's his game then? Does he suffer
from sculptor's block? Does he maintain
a museum rather than a gallery? Does he
despise commerce?

Maybe he knows he's carved one
perfect rose and one perfect goldfish and
he is waiting for all Paris to celebrate that.
Why are they taking so long?
Must his art rot and must he die?
Well, that is the tradition.

SIDNEY SAYS (DO THIS)

no offense   sidney says
but who the hell needs poems
look   what can a poet tell me
about a sunset for instance
that i can't see for myself

sidney   every sunset i see now
i see your big red worried face

FRAME OF REFERENCE I

The race is on
For every name I can't remember
from the old Dodgers' catcher
to that editor on the Trib
there is an abundance of names
readily springing to mind
that anyone younger than I am
doesn't recognize
What to do?
Resort to footnotes?
Identifying parentheses?
Mary Astor was a movie star
Eddie Kranepool played first. First what?
Walter Lippman wrote a column
Where to draw the line? Franklin Roosevelt
was a president of the United States
Faulkner wrote books
Honey, you look just like Veronica Lake.
No, that's a person, not a place.

FRAME OF REFERENCE II

for Russell Freedman

One day it became clear that "according to
Emily Post" no longer means anything to anyone
under fill-in-the-blank age, that she has been rudely thrown
out of the language and people who lack her guidance
are cutting wedding cakes with salad forks and
sending sympathy cards with smiley faces

And if Mrs. Post has melted into anonymity
into the swamp of footnotes and parentheses
what chance is there for Cookie Lavagetto or
Drew Pearson or Vilma Banky or Douglas Haig
or Juanita Hall or Cordell Hull or Virginia Hill
or Peaches Browning or Eric Golden or Lester Lanin
or Vincent Impellitieri or Ben Blue or Pumpsie Green
or Westbrook Pegler or Sweetwater Clifton
or Gus Lesnovich or Freddie Batholomew or Porfirio
Rubirosa or Birdie Tebbets or Wendy Barrie or
the day after tomorrow, you
and me

D-Day? she said, what's D-Day
never heard of it
He (amazed) How could you not know
about D-Day, blah blah blah June 6, 1944
She (indignant) Jesus Christ! That happened
before I was *born!*

DEAD RED

Where have all the redheads gone?
Have they retreated in rage and disappointment
to a commune in the Red River Valley or
hidden themselves under giant fur hats
as they stumble around Red Square?
Red Buttons and Red Barber, Red Skelton
and Red Ruffing, all dead, long dead --
And no new Reds to replace them
        Excuse me, do you know anyone
named Red? You say you don't know
What I'm talking about? Well,
then maybe you can tell me
Where did all these whitebearded
 bald guys come from?

LUNCH WITH VIRGINIA

On the way here, I offered my seat
on the F train to a guy carrying a basketball
and I offered to help a very important executive
cross Fifth Avenue, cautioning him to look both ways
I told some lies to those grandmas at the corner table
so they would stare disapprovingly at you while complaining loudly
about these kids today and the young couple in the booth --
let's ask if they need help reading the menu's tiny type
Later we can stare down cab drivers and menace
bike messengers and elbow people into puddles
So: what looks good today?

FRYING

hamburgers frying
in the dark

everyone's
separate life
a mystery

FOR ROSE PERNICK ON THE 100th ANNIVERSARY OF HER BIRTH AND THE ALMOST IMMEDIATE ARRIVAL OF DISCONTENT

After she had finished calling every relative
who would still listen,
to tell them Sue and I had stolen all her money
and when she was finished firing that week's
domestic helper (who she thought was stealing)
Mother launched a new campaign
She called everyone she could think of
to say that her life would be torment unless
she could have a white cardigan but,
alas, she could not afford to buy one
(since Sue and I had stolen all her money)
And my sister, a lover of family who would
never say uncle, heard this heartbreaking appeal
and was soon on a plane to Fort Lauderdale
with a fine white cardigan in her bag.
And when she arrived at the condo, after
the exchange of wary greetings,
she went into the bedroom, and there
overflowing on the dresser-top,
were piles of cardigans, towers
of cardigans, prodigies of cardigans,
a snow-capped Everest of
twenty-three white cardigans,
sent by the kindly and gullible,
and still virginal in their wrappings.
But Mom – all these sweaters,
what will you do with all these sweaters?
Ha, Mom replied, shiny-eyed
in her bottom-line glory:
Do you think I'd wear any of this crap!

POWDER

No one respects the wishes of the dead
He who wanted to be encased in walnut
and laid in the ground
with his wife's grandmother
is burned to a crisp
and dispensed as a powder
Do not publish my letters, the dead insist
Do not sell my horses
Do not re-marry a gentile, a Chinese
a Mormon or a dwarf
But no one listens to powder

THE FIFTH OF JULY

It was the second coldest second rainiest
Fourth of July ever said the forecaster looking back
Nearly all celebrations were canceled but
I believe that if I sit in a strange bar in
Minnesota or Maine and watch the door hard enough
someone I love will come rushing in and
we will cheer and embrace
Insane optimism has got me this far
But watch those swinging doors, my dear

A man in the bar is furious at the government
for changing the date of Veterans Day
as though he'd witnessed the armistice in 1918
But they wouldn't mess with the goddamn fourth he said
        Only a few drunks out in the rain last night
trying to get the spark to catch
not understanding the day had sputtered out

And they have my full support, slipping in the mud
I am an upright citizen, I believe in progress
I believe in fallacious concepts of romantic love
I believe in bankrupt theories of cinematic inevitability
I believe in triple features as anaesthesia
I believe the sodden wick might just catch

        I believe in testimony by anecdote:
Harold Ross's favorite reporter resigned
from the New Yorker to go to Hollywood
Ross was overcome. All he could say was
God bless you McNulty goddamn it

POPULARITY

1.
I could hardly wait to get to the party!
I had news of the death of everyone's best friend!

2.
God was I funny I was terrific
I wanted the words to spin so fast
everything would stand still
I wanted to tear off their faces
and spit in their blood

THE WRONG WAY TO REMSEN STREET

for Carol Baum

ten years ago in downtown brooklyn
a man asked me how to get to remsen street
and i gave him the wrong directions
i have regretted it ever since

i have learned to live with that guilt
inattentive
rushed
selfish
unfeeling
deaf to a stranger's urgent need to find
remsen street where in all probability
a close relative lay dying
straining to stay alive just a minute more
long enough to whisper the combination of the safe
to the one man the only man worthy of that trust
the man i sent two blocks forward
instead of two blocks back
ten years of torment seems a small price to pay

what i have come to question
is the assumption of faith in my own credibility
never once in these wasted shadowy years
has it occurred to me that
he might not have followed my directions
he might have checked with someone else
who sent him the right way or at least
would bear the final blame for the wrong way
which is nearly as good

actually i have assumed his faith to be unwavering
by now   walking in a straight line
he should be passing through boise idaho for the third time
covered with red leaves and seashells
every few miles he stops
rubs his feet mops his brow squints in the sun
suddenly he is filled with doubt

should he have listened to the woman
who told him to go past the bank
and make a right at burger king?
is remsen street not over the next hill?

then he puts his hat back on
and takes the first impossible step
toward Pullman Washington

NEW YORK LIVERY

It is a grand thing that a man
so recently arrived from Albania
can find himself already behind
the wheel of a dented Lincoln town car
Now we must teach him that LaGuardia
and JFK are not the same place, that Grand
Central Terminal is not on Grand Central Parkway
If he chooses to go from Morningside Heights
to Staten Island via the Queens Midtown Tunnel,
however, that is his right of self-expression
and shows he is no slave to geography

RICH, STUPID, AND CRAZY

Being rich
makes you stupid
If you haven't tied
your own shoes
in twenty years
you don't know how
to tie your shoes

Being crazy
makes you stupid
Your start to pour
the coffee and
the roar of the beast
in your eye
startles you and you
pour the coffee
into your shoe
and then you
enter the maze
that leads to why
that's a good idea

Most Americans
know lots of stupid people
but not many rich ones
I mean horse farm
seagoing yacht
flat in London
townhouse in Paris
20 room condo with
library chosen by
the interior decorator
rich
not the local dentist
with three cars and
a house at the lake

But crazy people
are easier to find
Some mornings I see

five or six before
the train reaches
Delancey Street
and this may be a
widely held opinion
on the F train
except not the same
five or six

Above ground
the stupid rich people
flood their limos with
lime juice and drown
with their perfect noses
pressed against
the rear window
And the drivers
just keep on driving

Down below
the gentle voices of
high school girls
What are you, stupid?
What are you, crazy?

NOSTALGIA™

At Uncle Li's
Golden Lotus New
Peking Tea Cup
I order pork egg foo yung
my father's favorite
fake Chinese food
and I eat it with a fork
off a chipped
blue and white plate

Then I light a Chesterfield
and go off to
register Republican

Save me

A PACK OF LUCKIES

I went out to get a pack of Luckies
Then I remembered that
I don't smoke anymore (although
I try to smolder occasionally)

so I couldn't disappear for 25 years
and then turn up
as a farmhand in Calgary
for the touching reunion with my
six children and their spawn
They forgive me, etc., as flashbulbs
pop

but none of this ever happened
because of my life-affirming
abstinence
How long was I really gone?
The frying pan
is still warm in my hand
and I'm breathing in
and out
and who has forgiven what?

MACHO MADNESS

for Mike Stegman

the exquisite summer pleasure
of pissing a mosquito to death

THE SIGN IN THE WINDOW OF THE IMPORTED CHEESE SHOP: STOP THE JAIL

After years of dust
and darkness
the Atlantic Avenue jail
is being restocked
with prisoners
but there are no more
views of parking lots
and broken bottles
Now there are glass towers
with Juliet balconies
and Ophelia lap pools
and Lady Macbeth sinks
and garages
where flaming BMWs
spiral down
to the pits of hell

And the condo owners
stare down
at the visitors' line
counting the brown
sisters the brown cousins
the brown brothers
the weary brown
grandmothers
and they calculate
the effect on their
real estate
Stop the jail, they cry
(or hide it underground)

GROWING UP GROWING OLD
GOING AWAY DYING

These are the houses on these blocks in Flatbush which have basketball hoops affixed to their garages.

On the east side of East 29th Street, between Avenues M and L: 13 houses have no basketball hoops, 3 have. Of the latter, one has a net and one is very rusty.

On the west side of East 29th Street, between Avenues L and K: 19 houses have no basketball hoops. Two houses do have hoops and both have nets. One house without a hoop has wooden supports erected, ready to hold up a backboard, and a box labeled "Superstar Backboard, Goal and Net" lying next to the garbage cans. At another house, without a hoop, a basketball lies on the ground near the back door.

East side of East 28th St., between K and J: 25 houses without hoops, 3 with, one net. Nothing remarkable.

West side of East 27th St., between J and K: 17 houses without hoops; one has a backboard without a hoop. Three with hoops. No nets.

East side, East 27th, between K and L: 13 houses without hoops, 2 with hoops, 3 with hoops and nets. One netless hoop very crooked.

Avenue L, north side, between East 27th and 26th Sts.: 4 houses without hoops, one with hoop and net. A man taking out the garbage sees me making notes in front of his house. What's up, he asks. Sorry, I'm not allowed to discuss it, I frown, and scribble an extra page.

West side, Bedford Ave., between L & M: 16 houses no hoops, one with hoop, one with hoop and net. One backboard barely visible over top of van in driveway; impossible to determine whether hoop and/or net in place.

South side, Avenue M, from Bedford to East 21st: 6 houses without hoops, 3 with hoops and nets, many houses without garages.

At this point, Avenue M becomes a commercial street and there are no more garages or houses. On every street surveyed, there were always more basketball hoops on the other side of the street.

MAY COMMA MERRY MONTH OF

Now you take your mayfly
Lives just one day
Born without a mouth or a stomach
Gets no nourishment

And it might not be a nice day
Maybe that one day
is in Troy NY in the snow
and in mayfly eternity
if somebody asked
what's it all about anyway?
a representative sample of mayflies
would say: Troy NY in the snow

Now I was born in May
and in my lifetime maypoles have disappeared
and parades have given way to drowning sailors
and maybe this isn't going to work out
Maybe every sailor drowns every time
Maybe the mayflies will forget May Day
right through Memorial Day
They'll scratch their tiny heads
and say what what who

It's true mayflies are also called june bugs
(no, it's not) and this argues for second chances
for coming in on a wing and a prayer
and maybe everything will be hunky dory
but there are no july flies

"RINSO WHITE, RINSO BRIGHT, HAPPY LITTLE WASHDAY SONG"

Duz does everything

Because the entrepreneurial spirit is
as unquenchable as it is unreasonable
there are three bodegas on the four corners
of this intersection
                              although now
that I look at the dusty boxes of Duz and
Rinso in the window of Vargas Gourmet
I suspect soap powder is not their major
source of income   A dime bag of
Oxydol, please

231: I COME TO THE GARDEN ALONE

The mockingbird in my backyard
never does car alarms or fire engines
He just does other mockingbirds
Where's the entertainment in that

The apple tree no longer bears apples
but we know it's an apple tree
because we have long memories
and signed contracts

The Rose of Sharon is 40 years old
It blooms every year like a birthday card
from an aunt with a relentless memory

Is the fence holding up the bush or
is the bush holding up the fence
Which side are you on?

LIKE SEAWATER

1.

in my neighborhood
during the worst of the heat
midnight looks like noon
whole families sit outside
in the dark
the men drinking beer
playing dominoes
the women talking on
the cracked steps
the babies playing
on the wet steamy sidewalks
fifty dollar cars roar
through the streets
through the jets
from the open hydrants
the gutters run as clean
as mountain streams
when it gets light
the men remain
talking quietly together
the taste of beer
in the morning
like seawater

2.

when my refrigerator was broken
i stopped at the corner store
on my way home from work
and bought two bottles of millers
knowing i could drink the first
before the second grew warm
the grocer without asking
put the bottles
in two separate brown bags
assuming i had a friend
waiting outside on the steps
why else would a sensible man
buy only two bottles of beer

EARLY HEAT

From the glare of July sun
into the shady delicatessen
clutching my mother's rolled-up
five-dollar bill which
I'd been pretending to smoke –
and suddenly Mr. Muller's
big red face
leaning into mine
and demanding of my
eight-year-old self
Hot enough for you!
which 1) scared the hell
out of me and 2) let me know
it was my fault, all of it

MORNING NEWS

As I puff my way up the subway stairs
at West 4th Street and finally reach
the air at sidewalk level
the man handing out copies
of a free tabloid,
just as I pass him, mutters
"What a mean face" and when
I realize he means me, that he can see me
as clearly as I can see him, I don't turn back
but I walk the blocks to my workplace
trying out a flip-book's worth of alternating
mean faces and benevolent smiles before
settling back into my natural expression,
much as you see me now

RICK'S LIQUORS

looks like any other liquor store
until you get inside and discover
that rick (rick   is that you?)
and all rick's bottles and cash
are behind plastic bullet-proof partitions
and there is no way you can get within two feet
of rick or anything that belongs to rick
we got tired of being ripped off
and locked in the can   says rick
sending your bottle down a little chute

MONAHAN

The City Edition and the Late City have both hit the streets and it's very quiet in the vast city room of the Herald Tribune, a few people on the desks, a few reporters reading or chatting.

As a copy boy without much seniority, I have drawn the late shift and I'm killing time until I can get out and catch up with the other guys. If it's a long time since payday, they'll be at the Show Bar on 41st Street, where the pressmen and the compositors hang out. If we've got a few bucks, we'll go to Jack Bleeck's, where the reporters and editors drink and people like Walt Kelly, the *Pogo* cartoonist, have been known to buy rounds for all Trib people.

Meanwhile, I am moping around, staring out the huge fifth floor windows. There's a big print shop directly opposite the city room, across 40th Street, that also goes all night. I'm used to seeing their windows all brightly lit. But tonight, I suddenly realize, it's not electric light, it's fire. The place is totally ablaze.

Now I'm fully awake. I go running across the city room toward the first authority figure I see. Mike Monahan, the grumpy old assistant telegraph editor (i.e. national news) is deeply involved in his paperwork.

"Mr. Monahan, Mr. Monahan!" I shout. "There's a huge fire across the street!"

Monahan never looks up. His pen still moving, he snarls: "That's cityside."

Was that even his name, Monahan? Morahan, Menahan. Eagan knew, but he's dead. Marty would know, but he's dead. Cathy O'Toole, are you alive at all, at all? McMenin, McMenamin. If I say it's goddamn Monahan, it's Monahan. Francis Xavier Monahan. Big Jack Monahan. Little Tommy Monahan. That roaring boy, that simpering toady, that twinkle-eyed old devil. If I say there's a fire, let the paper start to char.

Mr. Monahan, Mr. Monahan, etc. As I sound the alarm, he leaps up from his desk and almost instantly clutches at his chest. A strangled cry. He falls to the floor with a great thud. Massive stroke. Dead. Just then, the teletypes start clacking away. Eisenhower has had a heart attack. Albert Anastasia's been shot in a barber shop. The Boer War has broken out. The South has seceded. I take over the desk and go to work. The copy is pouring in from four machines at once, but my pace never slackens. Front page story after front page story. John Steinbeck wins the Nobel. Cigarettes cause cancer. Dean Acheson is parachuted over France. The city room fills, then empties, fills and empties. I man the desk for 48 hours, never standing once.

And that is how I became managing editor of the New York Herald Tribune at the age of seventeen. It's one for the history books.

CAPPUCCINOS

No, not the cappuccinos
suburban ladies get frothy
mustaches from after dinner
I mean the ones at Tosca
in North Beach, with brandy and
anisette in the coffee and cream,
just the thing on a raw San Francisco
evening and they go down like
chocolate milk and roar back like
a two by four to the temple
just when you were dancing so nicely
on the top of the bar. Well,
they're no good
if you let them get cold.
What is?

BEER AND WINE LICENSE

McKenna at the end of the bar
empty beer mug as collection box
Dusty sunshine doesn't reach his stool

All afternoon
Gus the bartender dumps
other people's leftovers
into McKenna's glass
Lucky Lager and Burgomeister
Hamm's and Coors and Carta Blanca
sweet vermouth and burgundy
and Seven-Up and Chablis

Finally McKenna's eyes begin to move
and he can lift the mug with one hand
Gus pours in a little sangria
Please   McKenna says
no cigarette butts

Which reminds Gus it's dusk
time to turn on the neon light

THE GOURMAND REFLECTS

I am the accumulated memory and waistline of the dead
restaurants of New York and the dishes that will never be
set before us again, the snow pea leaves in garlic at the
Ocean Palace, the blini and caviar at the Russian Tea
Room, the osso buco at the New Port Alba, the kashe
varnishkes at the Second Avenue Deli, the veal ragout
at C'ent Anni –

C'ent anni – May you live a hundred
years. Maybe just a figure, of speech. But do I hear
something bubbling, crackling, sizzling, boiling? There are
19,000 restaurants in New York, three meals a day for
6,333 days and then start at the beginning again, the
chance every time the menu opens, it's going to
say I love you.

TOURIST WALKED RIGHT IN

tourist walked right into my colon
came pouring out my ears
complaining about the prices

tourist wanted to buy my cousin
tie her to the bumper of
a gray line bus

how do you live here, the tourists
whined and shot us dead just to show
they ain't no hicks

wall of tourists blocks the sidewalk
bike messenger kamikazes
turn them into ohio jam

we're all new yorkers now, they said
let's see them step over a drunk
a corpse a flaming cab

a pile of shit a pool of vomit
a pile of pigeons a pail of piss and
eat a banana on the f train

NEW YEAR'S DAY

My friend puts down his wine glass and
sighs that he's the oldest person
in this noisy restaurant. If he suddenly
went up in smoke
then I would be the oldest person
in this noisy restaurant

On New Year's Day at the Poetry
Project, I look down the long list
of readers in the marathon, hours
and hours of readers. Where is
this one? Where is that one?
Dead, dead, dead or nearly so.

Am I the oldest reader? Wait,
there's Taylor Mead.
Eat your broccoli, Taylor Mead.
I'm counting on you

TWO OLD WOMEN WHO MAY

Two old women
who may be sisters

speaking what might be
Polish on a crowded subway

Sometimes they whisper

COPS

I saw two cops
dancing
in the moonlight
no, wait
it was one cop dancing
with his reflection
in a mud puddle
but the mud cop
was off the beat
so vertical cop
splashed heavily
now wears his
pain face on the
bottom of his boot

and is it true
the cops compete to
see who can run
the most red lights
in a year
yes, it is true
why?
because they can
why do they shoot
unarmed hedge fund
managers?

gene brook said
put an ad in the paper:
anyone who wants
to be a cop
come to room 202
and anyone
who comes
can't be a cop

I'M NOT A DOCTOR BUT

for Larry Fagin

I'm not a doctor but
I play one on
the 79th Street crosstown bus
and I'm very busy
I've covered all the little girls
in their school uniforms
with band-aids on their elbows
knees and noses
and I performed an appendectomy
on some old guy while
we went through the park
(no anesthesia but lots
of birdsong)
I had to amputate the driver's ears
but he's learned to love the quiet
My practice has doubled
between Madison and Columbus
I'm just very, very busy

WHAT I'M WEARING THIS DECEMBER DAY

I'm wearing big shoes
for heavy weather

Wigwam socks
Grandma loves you

Blue corduroy pants
thinning at the stress points

White boxer shorts
Tell *People* magazine

Flannel shirt
plaidness of my youth

Polartec jacket –
Marry me, fleece

Loden coat, fly to
Rome *now*

Borsolino cap,
the private eyes

It's snowing, I'm going
uptown for a fight

CATS AND DOGS

for J.

did you hear that
did you hear that
cats and dogs
cats and dogs
creeping up
on the house

did you hear that
cats and dogs
dance in the leaves
very slow
very quiet
cats and dogs
in the dark
dancing slow

did you feel that
cats and dogs
knock on the windows
cats and dogs
knock on the doors
cats and dogs singing slow
in the moonlight
and here they are
cats and dogs
knock on the door
cats and dogs
walking slow
through the halls
and here they are

here they are
on the bed
cats and dogs
warm your feet
cats and dogs
hold your hand

cats and dogs
stroke your hair
cats and dogs
singing in your ear
the tune that was on
the tip of your tongue
cats and dogs
walk up and down
walk up and down
that tender weight
that just-right weight

cats and dogs
stay all night
sleep slow
cats and dogs
in the morning sun
slow morning
cats and dogs
look in your eyes
good morning
they left their bags
and their bones
and their toys
just outside
in the slow morning
they'll stay
for lunch
they'll stay
for tea
they'll stay
for brandy and biscuits
and
did you hear that
they're singing again

BIG BLUE CHAIR

The reviewer was gushing that Mr. Alexie had just
published his 92nd book and he was only 29 years old
(or was it 29th book and 92 years old?) No, it was 29 years:
Why do they always have to carry on about my age?
complained the bright-eyed young author. Don't worry,
I explained (tapping out my pipe and setting fire to
the Irish setter) next year you'll be thirty and no
one will ever give a goddamn again

Which brings us to the present great occasion and luckily
I am still here to point the way

When I turned forty, I sank deep into my big
blue chair and began a careful study of the Hogarth
print on the opposite wall, counting every crosshatch
and waiting for the little dog to move. I congratulated
myself on the grace with which I was facing this
dramatic occasion, the great calm I was imposing
on my turbulent and disorderly life. I settled
deeper into the big blue chair

and then three months later
I stood up

GEORGE GREEN HAS HALF A HEADACHE

George Green has been walking around with half
a headache for hours now, determined not to gobble
down two Tylenol, lest those be the two Tylenol that
put him over the top, that break the camel's back
(and the camel will require Percocet but that's his lookout)
I share the apparent concern that the residue of 10,000
Lifetime Tylenols has just been mounting inside the body,
filling it like white goo in a baker's mold,
and these last two will reach the saturation point at the neck
and leave me standing immobilized in the middle of Seventh Avenue
near the chalky George Segal sculptures, as cab drivers shout
curses that would mean automatic knife fight in their homelands.
At least this may explain why I find myself avoiding strenuous
exercises like getting up from sofas and bending over
to pick up money on the sidewalk. Hell, it was only a five.

Life was simpler once, he creaked. No Tylenol, no Aleve,
no Excedrin. Just aspirin.
In the Fictitious Forties, I ran home from school
to bring the news to my mother: You don't have to spend
a lot of money on Bayer because A) all aspirin is the same and
B) Bayer used slave labor in the war, the Nazi rats.
But she was going to stick with Bayer
"because I know it's clean."

So George is still walking around with his head
split down the middle. Which side hurts? Maybe it's
the right brain, trying to push out a poem, so if you
offered him even half a Tylenol, you'd be murdering his art.
Can't do that. Luckily, he's braver than brave.
Good man, George. Keep on throbbing.

DISTANT NOTES

i try to capture the melody
to make it make sense
i want the tune hummable

someone is dusting a piano

SILENCE

Now I'm never going
to learn how to whistle or
make that sound
of a bat hitting the ball
or the way the creaking door
on "Inner Sanctum Mystery"
sounded on the radio, floating
across the apartment from
my parents' bedroom into
my room where I lay terrified
but attentive. Now I can do
that trick in silence.

FROM A SUNFISH

When we could no longer see the swimmers
we could still hear their voices
the father's calm instructions to his sons

SECRET HANDSHAKES

If you don't make a choice, the choice chooses you.

Now I belong to the group of people who have sat on
their reading glasses. They make eye contact on the F
train and offer secret handshakes, just as the people
who wear their scarves under their coats
try to convince me to join the conspiracy to push
the people who wear their scarves over their coats
out into the traffic or at least the deep slush.
It's all very subtle, the desperate pleas from the black
coffee drinkers to join in the struggle against three
sugars extra light
                        and now the wrinkled ones
with the gray eyes come and stand around me in
silence. I bought new glasses, I can switch to tea,
but I feel the crowd growing and when I turn
I know them all, every one.

THE LONE RANGER

She says print out some copies so
I Xerox a few copies
I make a few carbon copies
I type up some true copies
I scribble a note

She says shoot him an email
I run to the corner phone booth
and close the door against the cold

She says turn on the dishwasher
and I reach for Harold's bar of brown soap

It's on HBO, she says. I try
to tune in the station, clear the static
There it is --
Return with us now to the thrilling days
of yesteryear

HOTEL LUCCHESE, ON THE LUNGARNO, 3 AM

I meant to walk past the window
and return to bed
but here I stand looking out
at the silent street
and the barely moving Arno
(with the occasional jagged branch)
and the hills beyond reaching toward
San Miniato and then on to the moon
everything still
and the years pass and I am
still standing there
still there
as though nature had planned
this reward for an old man's
urgent nocturnal risings and
I'm still there
still here
still there

WAITING FOR THE LIGHT TO CHANGE

I like those mixed nuts at Costco and I don't
mind going so much if the checkout lines are short
and they're supposed to be very good employers
but Wegman's is supposed to be even better
but they're not in the city, they're in western
New York, which I know from our many trips
to Buffalo in our old Toyota and I don't know
if I'd get another Toyota after all the recalls but
we won't be going to Buffalo anymore anyway
because Myra Brook, of the sweet tooth and
contagious giggle, has died at the age of 88 and
now her ashes are buried in our backyard under
the bushes of yellow knockout roses
planted by Galen and her sturdy sons who were
accompanied by Atticus, age five, who rescued
the earthworms and put them in the box
that the ashes came in
And now the honking behind me
says the light has changed

LURKING

I've been 75 now
for 72 hours
and I'm still waiting for
my big break
I thought I saw it
lurking
in a dark doorway
across the street
but a bus blocked
the view
and when it passed
all I saw was a heap
of black bags awaiting
New York's Strongest
(which we all aspire to be)
sweaty men in faded t-shirts
clearing out the dripping trash
(which we all aspire to do)
I'm ready to dash
across now
All I need is a break
in the traffic

A BLUE SHOVEL

at three o'clock this morning
i became obsessed with the idea
that no one ever thinks about me
unless i am standing right in front of him/her/them
which is why i have to do it all myself
and never have time left over for composing oratorios

i put this theory to certain proofs
first, i counted to 1,060 fifteen times and the phone
didn't ring even once   then i called 49 people
selected scientifically to include a full range of
close friends and people i went to grover cleveland high school with
and not one of them said: hey, i was just thinking about you

                    that list (he paused dramatically, the audience
shifted in their seats and coughed nervously) that list
included several people in this very room
          (again the audience stirred, there were groans: o my god
          in the back of the room a man rose from his seat
          then saw the door was guarded)
well, i want you to know i forgive you
it may not even have been your fault
i may have been giving off fumes of some sort that induced amnesia
so that no sooner would i finish saying
the matisse drawing i bought for you is in the next room, i'll just get it
than you would be thinking who was that masked man? why is that
          curtain rustling?
what was i going to do with these eggs?

so i'm changing everything
i'm going to be quieter looser denser taller faster closer to cold water
than a blue shovel tighter noisier dancing the new steps two three
various touchstones will be skimmed across the lake
so that the last time you heard me tell you
about my being the only person you'll meet this year
who has been the guest of honor at a rotary club luncheon
in valdese, north carolina, a town founded by descendants
of the waldensian heresy who have all become manufacturers of
          pantyhose
was the last time   except for this time

and there's just a hint of a written excuse from the family doctor
for this time: please excuse his absence from your presence
he's always been difficult to envision in a particular place

at any rate, the doors are still barricaded
so you might as well get a head start on memorizing my life's work
i'll wait till you're through i'll just stand right here

THE ANSWERS TO THE QUESTIONS

For that rainy day reading at
the bookstore in the mall

Where do you get your ideas?
From a guy named Howie in Philadelphia.
They're $19.95 a dozen, less if they've been used.
I used to get some from my family's horrible holiday
dinners, but they won't let me in the house anymore

Who are your influences?
Any number of colorful obscurities whose
names you feel bad about not knowing
and this is because
I am inventing them as I speak.
And Frank O'Hara.
You always have to say Frank O'Hara.

When do you put in the hidden meaning?
I usually write that first, then cover it up
with mud and leaves so that it's totally
obscured, then I forget where I put it so
your guess is as good as mine. You can
bring your own meaning and just slather it on.

Can you stay for the open reading?
I'd like to stay, I really want to stay
I'd do anything in the world to stay
I've dreamed of staying,
I would have definitely stayed but
now I've fallen into past tense so
I'm afraid it's impossible to climb out.
And I think there's a terrible storm coming.

What is that buzzing sound?
I wonder if I'll get home faster if
I get on Route 80 and take the bridge.
I see myself speeding down a deserted highway
What *is* that annoying sound? Oh.
It's me. I seem to be reading.
I wondered why they turned the music off.

STAY HOME

What is the finest thing one friend can do for another?

Cancel a dinner date. (Let's stay home.)

And how can you repay that thoughtfulness?

Don't go to his reading, avoid her award ceremony, forget the opening.

(We'll just stay home.).

If luck holds, the play you bought tickets for six months ago will get terrible reviews and close on the second night.

You'll not only get to stay home, you'll get money back.

That movie came and went and the theater is now a Walgreen's.

We'll stay home, take some Tylenol.

Stay home, stay home. There's just the rain. Everything else is silence.

Silence. Shhhh.

(Silence.)

AFTERWORD: GRANT AVENUE

I moved to San Francisco over fifty years ago. It wasn't for the poetry.

In 1957, I had a degree in journalism from New York University and two years' experience as a copy boy and editorial assistant with the New York *Herald Tribune*. I was ready to take my place in the dashing, hard-drinking world of reporters. All that Hildy Johnson/ *The Front Page* stuff had been conscientiously debunked at NYU, but at the Trib, the financial copy desk always had a bottle of Scotch on the table and Al Laney, the old hockey writer, always wore his fedora in the office. That did it for me

I wanted to write news, race deadlines, get scoops, hang out in bars. I lived at home, in Queens, while I was in school—it's hard to believe that NYU, the monster that has swallowed lower Manhattan, had no dorms in those days—and I was eager to get as far away from New York as I could.

Tom Eagan, schoolmate and fellow copy boy—copy boys on major metropolitan dailies are not boys; they often have master's degrees— had moved to San Francisco a year before and kept writing me letters about the wonder of it all. I didn't need a lot of convincing. I flew out there in September, 1957, thinking I'd stay a few months maybe (but that turned into five years, which is very Californian.) I arrived on the opening day of the "Howl" obscenity trial. Of course, it didn't mean a thing to me. My total lifetime poetry experience at that point centered on having to memorize "Miniver Cheevy" and a part of "General William Booth Enters into Heaven" in high school where my English teachers otherwise did a very effective job of passing on their own terror and hatred of poetry. I imagine there must have been a few others, but....

Eagan's small apartment happened to be on Filbert Street and Grant Avenue, right in the middle of North Beach. I thought I'd sleep on his sofa for a week or so, but that turned into six months. Tom was working as a reporter for the *Examiner,* in their Oakland office, and didn't like it. I had $500. So he quit his job and we had a good time until the money ran out and we were living on mayonnaise sandwiches. Tom was one of those people who never adjust to the cool, damp San Francisco weather. There was a built-in gas heater in the apartment and he kept it on high. Every night, as the gas ate up the air, I'd conk out at ten o'clock, thinking, What an early town San Francisco is.

Tom had ended up in North Beach by accident and wasn't much interested in the neighborhood, but once I figured out that it was the gas heat not the city, I began venturing forth. The neighborhood seemed just right to me; every other storefront was a bar – The Place, The Black Cat, the Anxious Asp, Frank's, Gino & Carlo's, The Cellar, XII Adler Place, the Vesuvio Café, Mister Otis, the Coffee Gallery, the Bagel Shop, the Green Valley. I'm telescoping a few years together here, but there were always a lot more bars than grocery stores. And in North Beach, everything happened in bars. If you were getting married in the evening or being awarded the Nobel Prize or having your gall bladder removed, first you would meet up with all your friends in a bar.

At this time, the *Chronicle* seemed full of Beat this and Beat that. I didn't hear this as literary, just the popular press's tag for the current mode of bohemianism. Soon Herb Caen, the columnist everyone read every morning although everyone denied it, invented the much-hated word "Beatnik" – Beat plus Sputnik. That kind of lurid publicity brought more and more tourists to Grant Avenue, but it also built up a defensive solidarity among the North Beachers. The neighborhood, at the foot of Telegraph Hill, was quite small, but some people never left it.

Jack Goodwin, North Beach's resident composer, wrote an opera with an aria entitled "He has a full-time, daytime job," which was sung in tones of awe. I finally got one of those, reporting for a chain of commercial newspapers. My office was on Market Street, but as soon as I left work, I headed right back to the Beach. It rarely occurred to me to do otherwise. I lived a block up Telegraph Hill, three good-sized, unheated rooms for $75 a month. That sounds ludicrously cheap, but as a reporter I made $75 a week.

> in 1959 my apartment in north beach
> had split-rattan blinds and kandinsky
> posters scotch-taped to the walls
> and a table made from a door
> and a bricks-and-boards bookcase
> and a mattress on the floor
> and almost everything was painted
> flat black except for the little yellow
> desk I bought from good will

and I wrote my first poems sitting there
watching headlights curve down
the lombard street hill

(excerpt from "Poster," *How to Ride on the Woodlawn Express,* SUN, 1986)

That's how it still looked in1961, when I started writing poems.

Anyway, I spent very little time in my pad. Sometimes I dropped into Frank's Bar for a drink after work and didn't get home for two days. Even when I was at low ebb, in the back of my mind I knew I was a regular, a guy who could run a tab, who always knew the bartender's name, who could stand up to any obnoxious tourist, knowing Bad-Talking Charlie or Tiburon Don would back me up. And I quickly fell in love with the secret hip language. It's hard to believe that in the Fifties, if you said, "Fall up to my pad, man, we can turn on and dig some sounds," to the squares (good word "squares," abandoned too early), you might as well have been speaking Estonian.

So who was in the bars? The usual population of artists and writers, drunks and cranks, drifters and grifters, brawlers and jokers, sax players and pool players, remittance men and Reed College alumnae. More Runyonesque names – Hube the Cube, Gene the Scrounge, Charlotte the Harlot, Linda Lovely, Ron the Inept Lecher, Pretty Anita (who wasn't so pretty) and Ugly Anita (who wasn't so ugly.) Some of the artists actually made art; some thought about it from time to time. And I started meeting poets, but let them wait a minute. Here are some of the people who made North Beach, North Beach.

JOHN AND KAY

John was going to return the borrowed books to Lulu. He'd thrown away the dust jackets.

She might be pissed about that, Kay said.

What?

The dust jackets. She might have wanted then.

Shit.

He started taking the dust jackets off other books, at random, and putting them on the borrowed books.

That's no damned good, Kay said. Why the hell would she want them that way?

John turned red and threw the books down. What's the fucking difference? If she wants dust jackets, these are dust jackets.

He left the books in the middle of the floor and went to Gino & Carlo's and drank brandy and coffee. He bought an old Dodge from a man at the bar for fifty dollars and drove it to Stinson Beach.

A week later, he drove the car back. It ran out of gas and he left it on the sidewalk in front of I. Magnin and went home.

They enjoyed the party.

Kay painted herself blue for Halloween and decided she liked it, so she left herself that way for a while. She went to the Safeway with the baby in the stroller and she bought milk and cereal and avocados and burgundy and cookies and mayonnaise and she was painted blue.

She became less blue in stages. First her hands. Then her legs. Her back. Her face. If any blue parts remained, no one knew.

(*How to Ride on the Woodlawn Express,* SUN, 1986)

MAPES AND FRAKES

Mapes was taller. Frakes was wider. They were both taller and wider than almost anyone. They were also pretty smart, but they preferred to be big. That was a choice to be made.

Frakes was blacklisted for having been in the CP so he couldn't ship out anymore, but Mapes still did. He'd become a sailor because he was a folksinger and it seemed a logical progression. The first night out, someone shouted "Fire in the hold!" and he leapt up from the table to do his part. When he got back, someone had eaten his rice pudding.

But Mapes still observed romantic tradition by breaking up bars and bystanders when he was on the beach. One time he had been roaring for six days and even his best friends were stepping behind trucks when they saw him. He'd left a clear trail of smashed jukeboxes and punched-out salesmen and the cops didn't seem too eager to catch up with him, but they finally picked him up early one Sunday evening, just standing on the corner of Grant and Vallejo. He was finished and ready to rest, but when he found out that the cops thought he was Frakes, his feelings were hurt.

A few weeks later, he married his seventh wife. She got him a full-time job, had a baby, and made the whole family eat oatmeal every morning.

But Frakes was always there. He played chess, he drank beer, did a little this and that. He walked in the neighborhood and he was the strongest man in the world, with all the responsibilities thereunto appertaining. People were flattered when he remembered their names but hoped he wouldn't slap them on the back. Sometimes he worked as a bouncer at Vesuvio, sending surly college boys soaring over the pavement of Columbus Avenue. Mt. Shasta, Muir Woods, the San Joaquin Valley, the strongest man in the world.

When there was almost no one around who even remembered Mapes anymore, Frakes grew older and slower and became silent. He sat in the bar of the San Gottardo Hotel and stared at his change. One day a young cab driver who lived upstairs was in the bar making a lot of noise. Frakes told him to shut up. The driver said go fuck yourself. Frakes walked over and forced the man's jaws open and spit in his mouth. Once that would have been the end of it. This day, the driver went upstairs and got his knife.

(*How to Ride on the Woodlawn Express*, SUN, 1986)

So I started meeting poets. Now, you didn't walk into a bar and always find Ginsberg, Snyder, Whalen, McClure and Corso all sitting there like a matched set, any more than you would have found Picasso, Stein, Hemingway, Fitzgerald and McAlmon nailed into place for constant viewing. But there were some poets who were around. There was Bob Stock, who made sandwiches at the Bagel Shop and occasionally played bad trumpet. John Allen Ryan tended bar at The Place and went off by himself into the mountain wilderness for weeks at a time. He'd been one of the six proprietors of the Six Gallery, site of the famous "Howl" reading. David Meltzer sold used books at the Discovery Bookstore. I saw Helen Adam standing on a wooden crate, reading to a street-corner crowd at a Grant Avenue Street Fair. From time to time, I found myself talking with Lawrence Ferlinghetti in Vesuvio, across the alley from City Lights.

There was one common denominator: I never ever thought of reading a poem by any of them.

I got to know Jack Spicer strictly as another guy who was always there, wearing his ratty suede jacket as he sat hunched at the bar. He was a serious and knowledgeable baseball fan and we watched quite a few Giant games together.

The San Francisco papers were always declaring some moron or other to be "King of the Beatniks." If anyone could have lived up to that title, it was Bob Kaufman.

BOB KAUFMAN

I never called the police when I heard Bob Kaufman
getting beaten up in the alley behind the house in North Beach
since it was always the police who were beating him.
They loved the way he bit and kicked and
scratched and never gave up.

We were neighbors in 1959—
until I came home one night and saw his place had
no door anymore. The cops had paid a call. The floor
was an inch thick with trash and needles, and taped
to the wall was a delivery bag that said: For All Your
Drug Needs, See Your Neighborhood Pharmacist

This was the Kaufman who circulated a petition
to get Henry Wallace's name on the ballot in
West Virginia in 1948 and was arrested for jay-
walking or some such by a friendly deputy who,
as he threw him into the drunk tank, said
Hey boys—
I got a New York commie nigger kike for you.

Now the city of San Francisco has named a *street*
for him—an alley, indeed! —O this shameless old
whore of a city!

        On the day after he died I read
a NY audience an old poem of mine in which he appeared
standing on a curb, afraid to step off.
A man came up to me afterward
to bemoan Bob's untimely death. Untimely?
It's the bloody miracle of the century that
Bob Kaufman lived till sixty. So many people
seemed to be against the idea.

(*The German Lunatic,* Hanging Loose Press, 2001)

By now it was 1960. I had quit my reporting job and was collecting
$55 a week unemployment insurance, the highest in the country
and enough to get me through the week if I was careful. I'd fallen
into a comfortable routine: get up in late morning, read for a while,
wander down to the Green Valley for a mid-day drink or two, go
to see whatever Two Action Hits Daily were playing at the Times
Theater, roam around the neighborhood until the bars closed, eat
minestrone and shoot pool at Mike's for an hour, in bed by four to
rest up for another busy day.

I had occasionally been trying to chip off the rust and try my hand
at writing stories again. It wasn't going well. When I was eighteen, I
had published a story in L. Rust Hills' magazine *Quixote* and I thought
fame was just days away. That turned out to be the only fiction I ever
published.

Then, one afternoon—a little drum roll here, please—I had A
Thought. It was a lively thought and it wouldn't go away. I sat at
my Royal portable and typed out a paragraph or so. What the hell is
this? It's not an idea for a story, it's not a grocery list, it's not a letter

to Aunt Sally. But it's sort of fun. And short. So I wrote another one. Mercifully, these first efforts disappeared long ago and I can't remember much about them. Weather-related, I think.

I wrote about 15 of them that week and they almost instantly, without my really thinking about it much, stopped being paragraphs and started arranging themselves in lines. Then I did something incredibly stupid and brash: I took six or seven of the poems (for I had decided that's what they were) and submitted them to a magazine called *The San Francisco Review*. They came back in a couple of weeks, but with a note: Try us again. I know the gods should have erased me from the planet for this sort of effrontery, but I have often wondered over the years what would have happened if I hadn't gotten that note. Would I have just shrugged and moved on to something else? Something that actually paid the rent, say?

Instead, I sent some poems to *The Nation* and got a nice note from someone named Merwin. That night, at Gino & Carlo's, I asked Jack Spicer if he'd heard of this Merwin. That was supposed to lead to some dialogue. Merwin is such and such, why do you ask? Well, actually, Jack, I've been writing some poems. Have you? I'd like to see them. Pause. Say, these are brilliant, etc., etc.

So I asked him, do you know someone named Merwin? Yeah, Spicer snapped, already walking away, he's some fucking priest.

It was many years later, that it hit me; He thought I said *Merton*.

I wrote 60 poems that year, almost none of which have survived, thank heavens. Then *Antioch Review* took one and *Epoch* took another and I was a Published Poet. All these years later, despite my balding pate and white beard, people I've been introduced to at parties, after the host has blown my cover, still say, "Oh, have you published?" Would they ask a dentist in his seventies if he'd ever filled a tooth?